I0814814

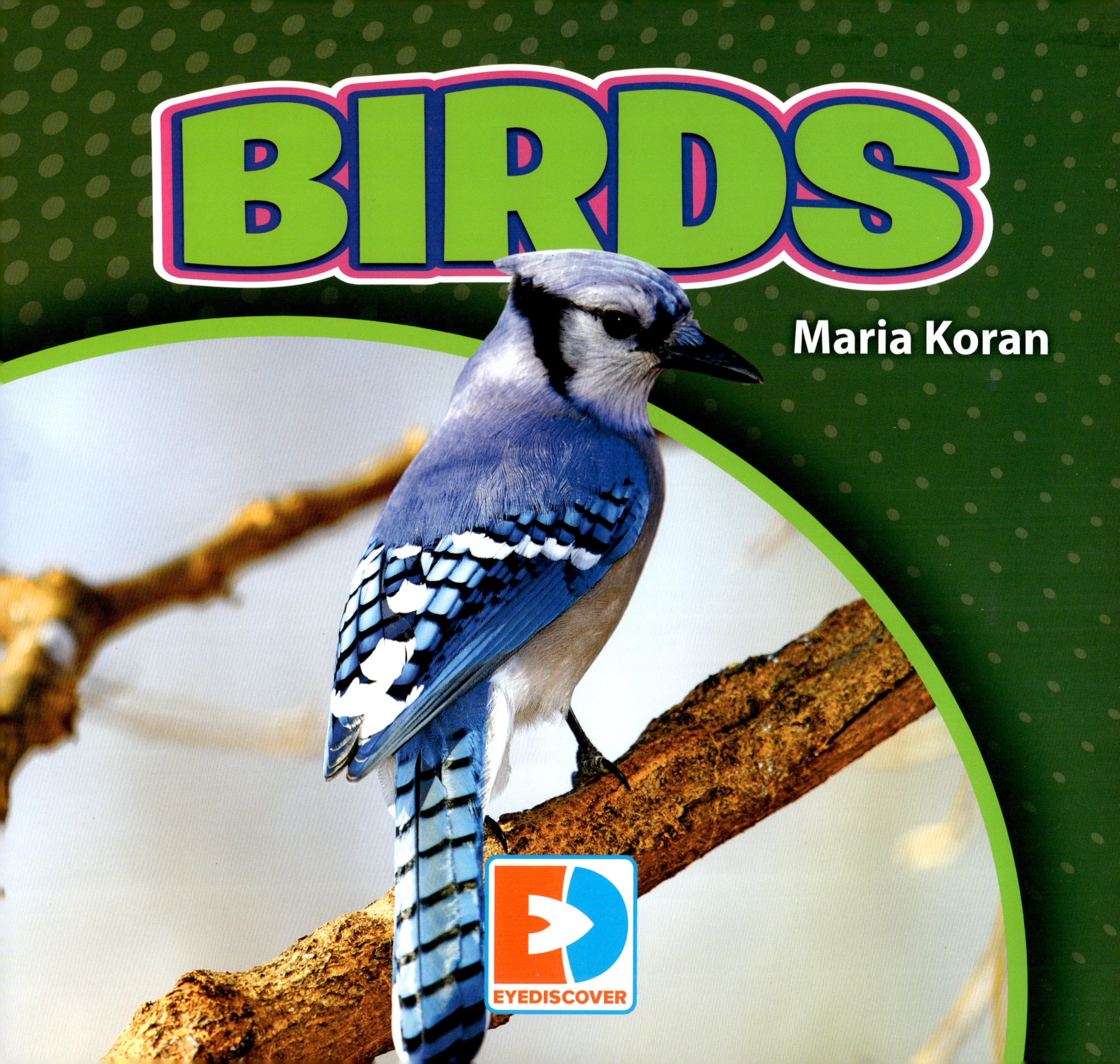
BIRDS
Maria Koran
EYEDISCOVER

Go to **www.eyediscover.com** and enter this book's unique code.

BOOK CODE

AVH43659

EYEDISCOVER brings you optic readalongs that support active learning.

Published by AV² by Weigl
350 5th Avenue, 59th Floor New York, NY 10118
Website: www.eyediscover.com

Library of Congress Cataloging-in-Publication Data available on request

ISBN 978-1-4896-8047-1 (hardcover)

Printed in Guangzhou, China
1 2 3 4 5 6 7 8 9 0 23 22 21 20 19

072019
121818

Project Coordinator: John Willis
Designer: Mandy Christiansen and Sushant Deshpande

Weigl acknowledges Alamy, iStock, and Shutterstock as the primary image suppliers for this title.

EYEDISCOVER provides enriched content, optimized for tablet use, that supplements and complements this book. EYEDISCOVER books strive to create inspired learning and engage young minds in a total learning experience.

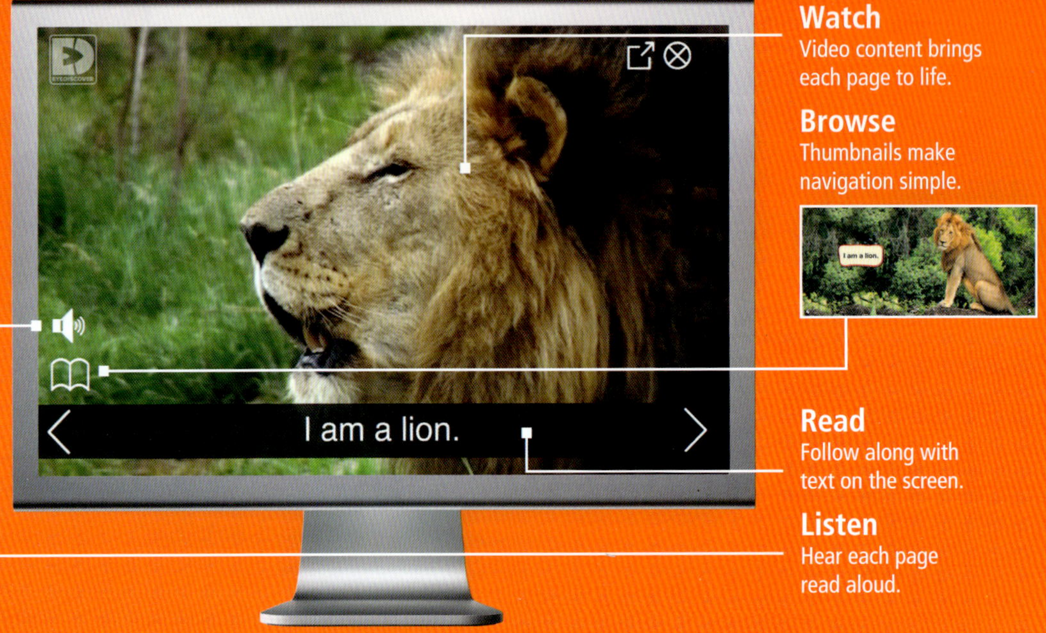

Your EYEDISCOVER Optic Readalongs come alive with...

Audio
Listen to the entire book read aloud.

Video
High resolution videos turn each spread into an optic readalong.

OPTIMIZED FOR

- ✓ TABLETS
- ✓ WHITEBOARDS
- ✓ COMPUTERS
- ✓ AND MUCH MORE!

In this book, you will learn about

- what they are
- what they look like
- what they do

and much more!

Birds are the only animals with feathers. Many birds use their wings to fly.

There are more than 10,000 kinds of birds. They live in every part of the world.

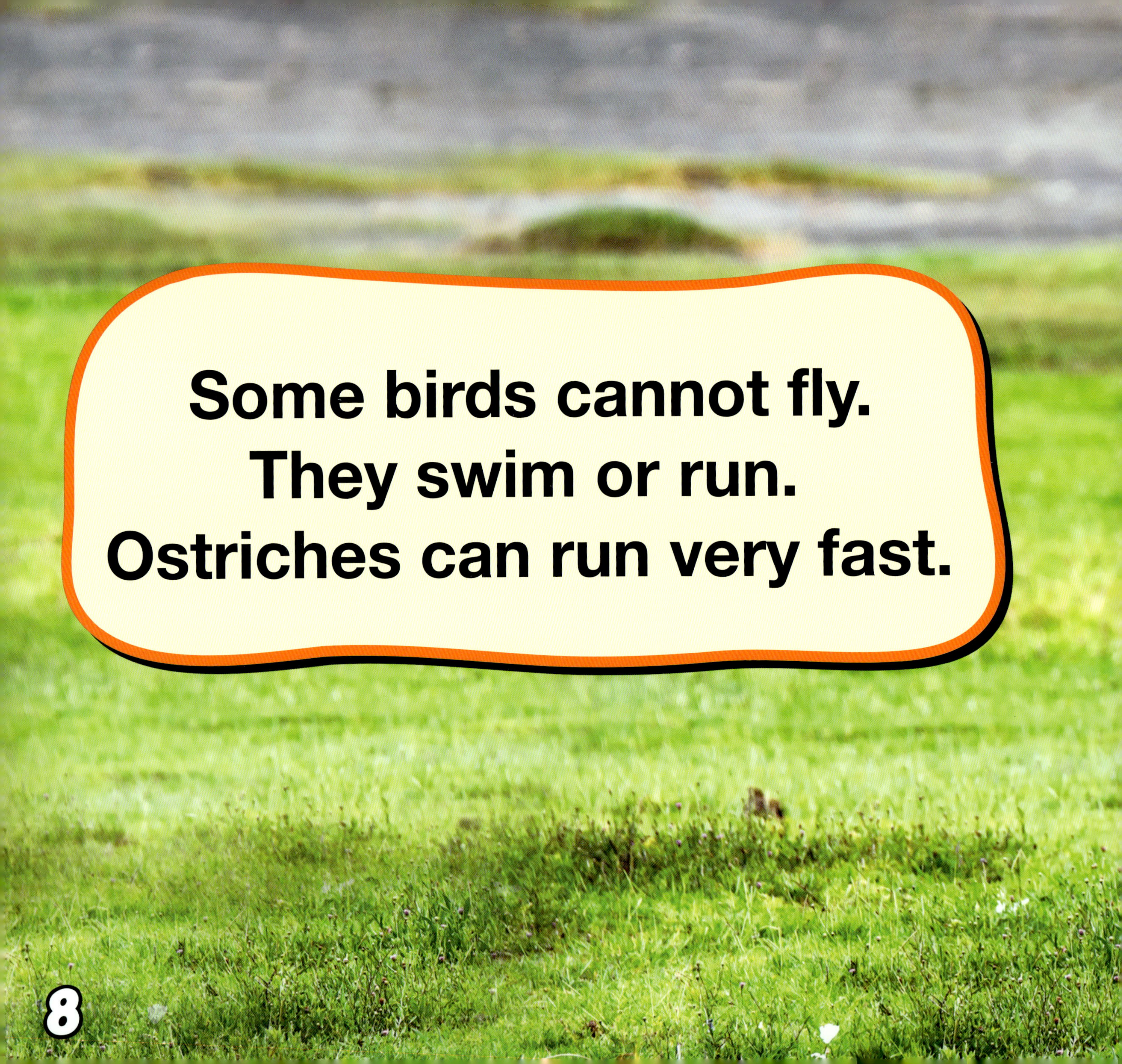

Some birds cannot fly.
They swim or run.
Ostriches can run very fast.

Hummingbirds can fly backward and sideways.

The bald eagle is a symbol of the United States. Most bald eagles live in Alaska.

Birds come in all shapes, sizes, and colors. Peacocks are known for their colorful tails.

Many birds sing. A wood thrush can sing two songs at the same time.

Baby birds are called chicks. They hatch from eggs. Chicks do not have feathers and cannot see.

People can help birds stay safe by keeping places that birds live in clean.

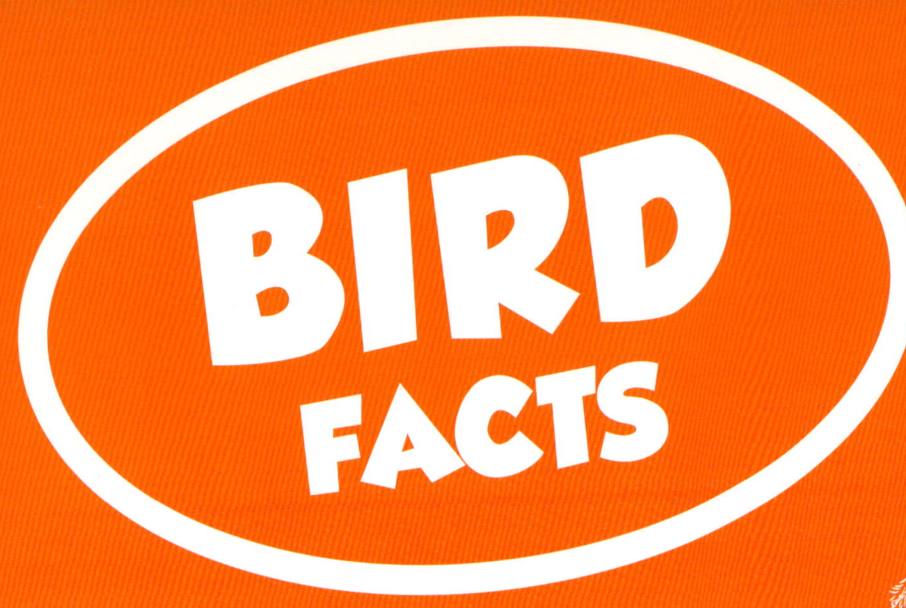

Ostriches are the **largest** birds.

Chickens
are the most
common **birds**.

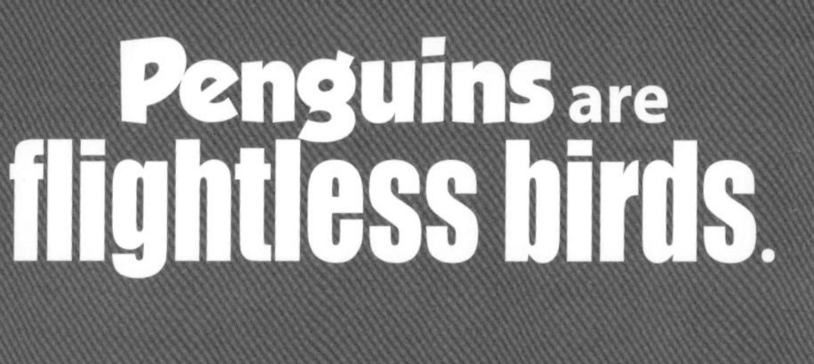

Penguins are **flightless birds.**

Birds have **hollow bones.**

Male birds are usually more **colorful** than female birds.

Birds live on every continent.

KEY WORDS

Research has shown that as much as 65 percent of all written material published in English is made up of 300 words. These 300 words cannot be taught using pictures or learned by sounding them out. They must be recognized by sight. This book contains 47 common sight words to help young readers improve their reading fluency and comprehension. This book also teaches young readers several important content words, such as proper nouns. These words are paired with pictures to aid in learning and improve understanding.

Page	Sight Words First Appearance
4	animals, are, many, only, the, their, to, use
7	every, in, kinds, live, more, of, part, than, there, they, world
8	can, or, run, some, very
11	and
12	a, is, most
15	all, come, for, known
16	at, same, songs, time, two
19	do, from, have, not, see
21	by, help, people, places, that

Page	Content Words First Appearance
4	birds, feathers, wings
8	ostriches, swim
11	hummingbirds
12	Alaska, bald eagle, symbol, United States
15	colors, peacocks, shapes, sizes, tails
16	wood thrush
19	chicks, eggs

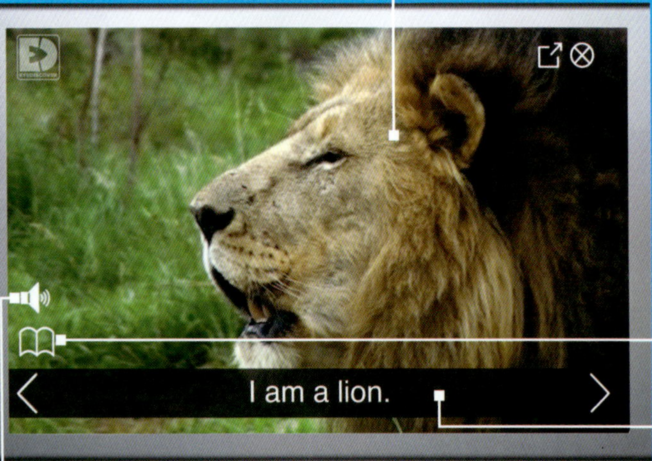

Watch
Video content brings each page to life.

Browse
Thumbnails make navigation simple.

Read
Follow along with text on the screen.

Listen
Hear each page read aloud.

Go to www.eyediscover.com and enter this book's unique code.

BOOK CODE

AVH43659